DRIVING WITH POPPI

Copyright © 2021 by J Thomas Brown

This is a work of creative nonfiction. All rights reserved. No part of this book may be reproduced in any manner whatsoever without written permission except in the case of brief quotations embodied in critical articles and reviews.

First published 2021 by FENGHUANG PUBLISHING

ISBN/SKU 978-0-578-80656-3 (Paperback)

EISBN 978-1-0879-2456-4 (ebook)

To connect with the author please visit www.jthomasbrown.com

DRIVING WITH POPPI

A Patremoir

J Thomas Brown

Fenghuang Publishing

CONTENTS

One	WANDERLUST	1
Two	THOSE WHO ARE GIVEN MUCH	9
Three	MGB	18
Four	BUCKS COUNTY	23
Five	LIES AND INNUENDOS	32
Six	TOO COLD FOR BUTTERFLIES	40
	ABOUT THE AUTHOR	51

One

WANDERLUST

My father was short but well-muscled, strong featured and well-formed. He was a clothes horse and dressed flamboyantly, but when it came to work was conservative and wore a dark three-piece suit. He was always in a hurry. Tears would appear in his shirts without explanation. Watch bands were replaced frequently, and cheap nylon straps substituted until the timepieces themselves stopped or the crystal faces cracked. His jewelry box was filled with watches: a Timex Expedition Indiglo with a broken backlight; an Omega Constellation Manhattan missing a strap; an unreadable Longines Automatic furrowed with gouges. He broke things: tools, door handles, radio buttons, knobs, steering wheels, and body parts, too.

I lived with my family on Tohickon Creek out in the countryside of Bucks County, Pennsylvania, at a gristmill built in 1758 called Sterner's Mill. In 1958 Sterner's Mill and the Tohickon Valley in which it rested were taken by eminent domain, the land denuded and our home bulldozed to create Nockamixon State Park and Recreational Lake.

As a nine-year-old boy, it was a magical place to live. The sound of the creek spilling over the millpond dam and millrace played through the air. A mossy coolness hovered along the creek like an ancient Lenape spirit. One-time Dad took me on a hike up the creek. We picked our way over boulders along the banks to where deserted hobo shacks poked through the woods on the opposite side. Much of that stretch of Tohickon Creek is a channel on the bottom of Lake Nockamixon today.

Dad seemed not to feel pain. He was digging a vegetable garden in the field out in back of the house when he ran the prong of the cultivator through his toe. He came into the house and removed his sneaker. I watched him apply mercurochrome and a bandage without flinching and then put the bloody shoe back on. He seemed unaffected and took me with him to buy seeds for the garden. I often wonder if he had a congenital pain insensitivity. From time to time he burned himself or cut his fingers and did not react other than to apply salve or band aids. Or perhaps pain was only a distraction better left ignored. To me, he always seemed indestructible.

Whether he was immune to pain or just decided not to waste his time with it became a moot question. Our delusions of immortality betray us all in the end.

Months before my father died, I asked him if he minded me writing about some of his colorful moments and driving exploits. There will be poking fun at your driving, I warned. He was a mensch about it.

Dad at the wheel was terrifying at times. We tried to laugh it off. If you drove with him, you might compare him to Mr. Magoo. But it was a mental thing. His mind was always crunching away on something else. He was not mentally in the same place where his body was. Dad said on several occasions he wished he had become a college professor and not an engineer. He enjoyed getting in front of an audience and lecturing with near perfect recall of dates and facts. Eidetic memory? He sounded like he was reading from an encyclopedia on the inside of his head. He gesticulated dramatically when speaking. This is okay if you are giving a lecture, but not if you are doing sixty down the highway and take your hands off the wheel.

My father had driving tickets. Lots. More than once, he pleaded before judges to keep his license. His driving exploits started as soon as he and my mother bought their first car, a 1955 Hudson sedan, when I was five and my sister, Lydia, four. They began their married life in a basement apartment near the Loch Raven Dam in Baltimore, too poor to afford a refrigerator. Mom, whose maiden name was Ruth Groves, had worked part time as a mechanical drafter for the City of Baltimore to help with Dad's college books and pay the rent. The milk and butter were kept on the windowsill outside the living room during the cooler months until Dad was hired by IBM® and they could afford their first house and a set of appliances.

Mom told me about the Hudson when I was older. Dad never mentioned it. When they had their apartment, he took the train to work downtown on a punch card machine project at the Social Security Administration. One morning he found a lucky parking spot near the tracks. That evening he drove home and parked at the curb outside the apartment. "What happened to your door?" a neighbor asked. Yard workers had wired the rear passenger door on with coat hangers after a passing train tore it off. Dad hadn't noticed. The railroad company paid enough in settlement to buy a new car, a green and white Pontiac Star Chief.

The year before moving to Sterner's Mill, my brother Jeffrey was born. Jeff was built on the stocky side like my father and stole a lot of the attention away from my sister and me. Lydia, on the other hand, inherited more of Dad's personality and was good at explaining things and telling everyone what to do. The hallmarks of a manager. I turned out more like my mother – artistic, only taller.

Six months after Jeff was born, Dad got promoted and was placed in charge of a mainframe computer project at Bethlehem Steel. The Pontiac was traded for a silver '57 Chevy Belair station wagon. The car didn't have air-conditioning, so we usually rolled down the windows in the summer. It was a hot day when Dad took me with him to buy seeds for the garden. On our way to the nursery in Quakertown, at the intersection of RT 309 and 313, was a traffic light. A car stopped next to us to make a left. The driver yelled, "Thanks for cutting me off you jackass." Dad leaned out his window. "Who taught *you* how to drive?" Not a zinger, but he held his ground. He glanced at me. I sat there blank faced, unsure if this was normal driver talk. The light changed and the other guy got in the last insult. "Asshole." That didn't feel normal.

Dad was always in a hurry, especially to get to business appointments. Over the years he was summoned to appear in traffic court many times. He would accumulate the maximum number of points allowable by law, then be ordered by the court to take a remedial driving course or else lose his license. He took remedial driving programs in Pennsylvania, New Jersey, and Delaware. After taking the course in Delaware, he got another speeding ticket on his way to a meeting in New Brunswick, New Jersey. He had an instinct for getting second chances and pleaded to the judge to let him take it one more time instead of revoking his license.

Dad had the wanderlust and loved travel to the point of dromomania. We were a family of nomads, migrating up and down the U.S. coast from Baltimore, Maryland, to Stamford, Connecticut, to Mountain Lakes, New Jersey, to Bucks County, Pennsylvania (several times) and then down to Atlanta, Georgia. We lived in Sweden, in the Hague (briefly), and in England for two years. The moves often took place in the middle of the school year. I still dream of walking crowded school halls in Stockholm, unable to find my classroom. Another recurring dream I have is that I'm an actor starring in a play. The curtain rises and the auditorium is filled with students. I panic, realizing I haven't read the play and don't know my lines.

IBMers often joked that IBM© stood for "I've been moved," and in the World Trade Division this was even more true. We moved to Lidingö, Sweden, an island off Stockholm, from Sterner's Mill in Bucks County, Pennsylvania. The winter was bitter cold and when the Baltic froze over the Swedes drove out on the ocean and ice skated. Dad showed remarkable judgement and never ventured to take our heavy station wagon out on the ice. Christmas Eve was one I'll always remember. We were invited to dinner with the Talets, the family of the man Dad worked with at Svenska Handelsbanken to install the bank's first mainframe system. After the meal the grownups skoaled. We gathered around the Christmas tree and the candles were lit. Real candles. They sang hymns in Swedish, then the candles were extinguished. On the way home it snowed.

Christmas morning, we exchanged presents. I got a pair of cross-country skis and a pair of woolen mittens from Lapland. They were hand made of a fine grey wool and very warm. Years later, I gave the mittens to my son.

Dad planned to move us to Germany the next year. Lydia and I were taken out of the Swedish public school and put in Deutsche Schule Stockholm, the German School of Stockholm. Jeff was put in kindergarten at the Deutsche Schule. After school, I was tutored in the German language. The idea was that we would be more prepared for moving to Germany, but Dad was offered a better position back in the States and instead moved us to Atlanta, Georgia, after the school year began. Taking private lessons to learn German in a country that spoke Swedish was confusing to me. No reasons were given at the time. Years later I realized Dad was just climbing the corporate ladder, although at times I think it was another manifestation of his wanderlust.

My father was born a year before the great depression in 1928 and grew up during those hard times. When he was a boy, he cut the meats for customers in my grandfather's delicatessen. The delicatessen was a country store with a porch roof overhanging a gas pump by the side of the road in Linthicum, Maryland. There were a couple of rooms in the back where Great-Grandmother and Great-Grandfather Snyder lived. The store was in the front. A long glass deli counter held the meats. Rows of shelves stacked with bread, vegetables, and canned goods stood lined up neatly on a wooden floor that popped and crackled beneath your feet.

Dad sliced meat to make sandwiches and cut up cabbages to make sauerkraut. The cut leaves were placed in a barrel and brine added, then they took it to the basement to cure. The same for pickles. Dad was a frequenter of delicatessens the rest of his life and liked to make bagels with salami for lunch.

My great-grandmother sat in front of a kerosene stove in the living room watching country music shows on TV, waiting for the door chimes to signal customers had entered. Their customers were local people, and in the depression era, had little money. Sometimes they bartered fresh vegetables for store goods. Some wrote IOUs.

By the end of each week Great-Grandfather Snyder had filled the bill spike on his desk with IOUs knowing he wouldn't be repaid. It was his way to give back to the community. He placed the cash proceeds in a bag and stuffed them under my father's shirt. Dad rode the trolley to Baltimore and deposited the money in the bank. No one would think a twelve-year-old boy would be carrying enough cash to be worth robbing. You don't find stores like that today.

Sometimes Dad would be gone on business for a week or two. When he came home for a weekend, we treasured the time he spent with us. One evening, during one of my mother's kicked-up-a-notch Sunday roast beef dinners, Dad walked in the dining room scraping a carving knife and sharpening rod rapidly together, creating a rhythmic metallic sound. When Mom set the roast on the table, he bent over it, continuing to hone the blade. He gave a show worthy of a Japanese grill chef. You expected him to throw a potato up and slice it in half in the air, but we wanted to eat.

Finally, he carved. Ridged scars stood out on his first and second fingers.

"How did you get those?" I asked.

"When I was a boy, I cut the meats in my grandfather's delicatessen. The knife slipped."

"Yeah? Did the knife slip, or did *you* slip up?"

He gave me the evil eye and faked a lunge at me with the knife. I parried with a stuck-out tongue thrust.

Two

THOSE WHO ARE GIVEN MUCH

Our family history is murky on the male side. The bookshelves in my parents' home in Doylestown, Pennsylvania, are filled with family photos and the places they have been. Beneath a table lamp on the bottom shelf is a faded lithograph of a strikingly handsome man, Great-Grandfather John Alexander Brown, and Grandfather John Thomas Brown, Sr. In the picture, my grandfather Brown, the youngest of four sons, sits at age five on a windlass on the beach of the Maryland Eastern Shore dressed in a gown. One of great grandfather's arms curves around him, the other points out over the Chesapeake Bay into the unknown. John Alexander had a literary degree and recited poetry in the taverns of Baltimore and wrote letters for the illiterate. Family lore has it that his name was not Brown, but Lochleer. My mother told me, quite convincingly, that he had been convicted of consorting with the enemy. On his way to federal prison in New York, he escaped and hid in the deep South where he changed his name to Brown to elude the police. I was astonished to learn of this and researched our genealogy - but found no evidence to substantiate it.

My grandfather, John Thomas, Sr., grew up in a rough part of Baltimore known as Pigtown. In the early 1900s pigs were driven through the neighborhood streets to the slaughterhouse. My great grandfather was an abusive alcoholic who caused my grandfather's life there to be unhappy. Grandpop ran away to Glen Allen, Virginia, at the age of thirteen to escape his father. He supported himself by working at a sawmill until, at sixteen years old, he lied about his age to join the navy and became a machinist's mate, first serving on a battleship, then a submarine.

My father had a different trajectory than my grandfather, who was self-educated. Grandpop once remarked absent mindedly, "You couldn't tell that boy anything." Then he showed me a letter signed by the corporate officers at Baltimore Gas and Electric where he worked as the nightshift foreman, attesting to Dad's intelligence and good character and how much he deserved a scholarship to Johns Hopkins.

Dad had been placed in an accelerated learning program at Baltimore Polytechnic Institute and graduated from high school in 1946 at the age of sixteen, then was awarded a scholarship to Johns Hopkins Whiting School of Engineering. He had barely finished growing when he graduated in 1949. Dad abandoned his old seersucker suit for a dark three-piece when he was hired by Big Blue during the reign of Thomas J. Watson, namesake of IBM's AI supercomputer, Watson. He was their youngest salesman at the time.

My father liked to paraphrase John F. Kennedy (who had himself paraphrased from Luke 12:48): "Much is expected of those who are given much." Throughout his life he was the one in charge: the church treasurer, Special Equestrians of Bucks County treasurer, the president of the Lions Club, the Rotary, and Habitat for Humanity.

Dad was hard on automobiles and went through a lot of them. The Chevy was showing its age by the time we moved to Atlanta, Georgia. He took me with him to shop for a new car. We looked at Oldsmobiles, Buicks, and a Willis Jeep. After a few days of car hunting by himself he drove home in a 1961 Hillman Minx two-door convertible, the descendent of a long line of sexy British Minxes exhibited at motor shows on the stands of Thrupp and Maberley, a once noble coachbuilder. With a forty-eight-horsepower engine it got great gas mileage, but made a lot of noise while doing it. It was perfect for sunny Georgia, sunglass manufacturers, and the skin tanning cream industry.

We moved to Stamford, Connecticut, a year and a half later and arrived there by Minx with our ears ringing from the straining whine of the motor and flap of the convertible top. Mom and Dad rented an old New England red frame house built on huge boulders with a barn that hung over a massive rock left over from the Ice Ages. When Dad was away, often for weeks at a time, I painted baseboards, took out the trash, and drove the Minx up and down the driveway to protect the engine while he was gone. After returning home from a long trip, the car wouldn't start, and he decided to repair it himself and let me help. This was a time of bonding. I learned the difference between a Phillips head and flat blade screwdriver and what an open-end wrench was. Later, as the twilight darkened, we pushed the Minx back into the barn. He called a mechanic who spent the next day hunting for a set of imported Lucas ignition points to fix the timing. If the points are damaged, the spark does not arrive to the engine cylinders to fire at the right time. If Lucas made guns, wars would not start either.

In the summer of 1962, when I was twelve, my parents bought a house on Silver Lake in Yardley, Pennsylvania. The Minx delivered us safely to our new home, but the previous owner was still in the middle of moving his furniture out when we arrived. Dad had a way of popping his eyes at people when he got angry that was intimidating, but nothing could change the fact that we couldn't move in until the owner physically moved out. It was in the wee hours of the morning before our movers left and we crashed exhausted on mattresses thrown on the floor.

There were several boys my age on our street and I played football whenever I had the chance. After football we went to Schino's to play eight ball in the basement. Lisa Green, on Yardley Avenue, threw parties at her house in the rec room. I would bring over the Beach Boys *Endless Summer* and she played her collection of The Lovin' Spoonful. During the second winter on Silver Lake there was a cold snap and kids from all over Yardley showed up to play ice hockey.

Dad traveled extensively while we lived on Silver Lake. At home on weekends he worked in a makeshift office in the master bedroom changing room. He bought two short filing cabinets and placed a door on them to make a desk. The cabinets filled up and the top cluttered over with manila envelopes and folders. On Mondays he boarded a train at Trenton and disappeared for a week or two.

On Friday, November 22nd, 1963, President Kennedy was assassinated. We were sent home from school early that afternoon. The bus was quiet. Someone told me the president was shot, but I didn't really get it. I walked home from my bus stop in a cloud of gloom, not comprehending what an assassination was. Dad stayed home on Monday and I watched the funeral on TV with him. As the horse-drawn caisson made its solemn way to the Capitol Rotunda tears streamed down his face. That was the first time I saw my father cry.

Yardley was a happy period for my sister, brother, mother, and me. I felt like I finally belonged to a neighborhood. I had friends, made the honor roll, and was promoted to first clarinet in the school band. My parents entertained a lot. Some of Dad's friends had skipped a few rungs climbing the corporate ladder and he mentioned after one of the parties that a college friend had become president of a division at IBM World Trade Corporation. He worked longer at his makeshift desk until the early hours of the morning. The organized chaos of his office expanded across the floor. No sooner had the Beatles appeared on The Ed Sullivan Show, then we were off to the Netherlands.

I listened to A Hard Day's Night, England Swings by Roger Miller, and other popular tunes on the plane's stereo system on the way to Rotterdam Airport. We stayed in The Hotel Des Indies while in the Hague and never looked for a permanent residence. Dad's World Trade assignment in the Netherlands was short, lasting only eight weeks. He used the Hague as a base for traveling throughout Europe. Mom took my sister, brother, and me to Madurodam miniature park, the Mauritshuis art museum, windmills, and historical sites while Dad took care of business. The night before we left for London, he treated us to a rijsttafeln, dozens of Indonesian dishes served with rice and covered in peanut or coconut curry sauce, a leftover from the Dutch colonial empire.

Our move to England was complicated by a shipyard crane dropping the shipping container holding our furniture. Mom turned it into an opportunity to replace the bent and broken things with English antiques acquired at auctions. The English set the bar for an antique to be four hundred years old or more. She was able to get bargains on two-hundred-year-old grandfather clocks, tables and chairs, dinnerware and crystal, that were sought after in The States where it was difficult to find things over a hundred.

We house hunted in London, but the homes were gloomy and smelled like cabbage. Finding schooling was difficult. Canes of various thickness stood racked outside the headmasters' offices. It was not reassuring to hear that canes were hardly ever used anymore. The English schools would not allow me to enter the British education system; by the tenth grade the American school system was two years behind the English. The British students were preparing for O and A level exams and on a path to university or trade education. Lydia and Jeff were not yet beyond hope and were accepted into the system.

My parents fell in love with an eighteenth-century manor in Sundridge, near Sevenoaks, Kent. It was called Greystone Court and was divided into three separate homes. Greystones was approached from a single driveway leading to three separate courtyards in the back. The front was kept in its original state facing the beautiful Kent countryside. Our third of the manor had a huge expanse of lawn, a gazebo, and a sunken rose garden. A solarium opened onto a wide veranda overlooking hedged gravel paths. In America it was my job to cut the grass and rake the leaves, but I could not get the English lawnmower to start. There was a flame thrower to control the weeds which I managed to ignite. It incinerated half the main path but fizzled out and I never could get it going again. We let the weeds grow until forced to hire a gardener.

The living room was used to entertain Mom and Dad's friends and business associates. It had a sunken floor with an ornate fireplace and French doors opening out to the veranda. The bedrooms were on the second floor and we were one short. It was decided I would use the library on the third floor for my bedroom. The walls were lined with English history, mysteries, and contemporary literature, including the unexpurgated version of *Lady Chatterley's Lover* banned in the United States. I read it for all the wrong reasons.

New Beacon Boys School in Sevenoaks took my brother in. He did well and got good at soccer. "What do they say about losing the Revolutionary War?" I asked one day.

He cracked a grin. "They had to let us go because they were too busy ruling the world."

Lydia enrolled in Combe Bank Convent where nuns daily smacked the students' knuckles with rulers and dealt verbal blows. Before her first year ended, she and three other girls hopped on a double decker bus outside the school entrance and made it halfway to London before the nuns caught up with them and hauled them back. They nearly got away. All were placed on disciplinary probation. I am proud of her for being the ringleader of the rebellion. Dad was, too. She was a leader.

Far into the school year it was decided the best solution for me was a boarding school in Bury St. Edmunds, Suffolk, called Herringswell Manor International School. Boys were required to wear a blazer, tie, smart trousers, and leather shoes; girls a blazer, white blouse, skirt below the knees, and calf socks. No sneakers or dungarees.

The Sunday before I was due to leave, I convinced my parents I was old enough to buy my clothes myself. They gave me the money to shop in London at Selfridges. But this was the era of Swinging London, so I made my way to Carnaby Street instead and bought a double-breasted Edwardian pinstripe blazer and matching bell bottoms, a flowered shirt and paisley tie. And a pair of leather Mod boots with high heels. Technically it was a suit – and the boots were leather.

When I got back home in the evening Mom was upset. It was my first *you-did-what?* "Whatever possessed you to do such a thing? Your father will be furious. It's a good thing he isn't here right now." I imagined Dad's eyes bulging out of their sockets, but he had already left for the airport.

A few days after I started school, Mom dropped off a new blazer, pants, and shoes. I finished out the year dressed according to code, but ten pounds lighter.

When school let out in June, I returned to Greystones feeling like a stranger. That evening Dad returned from one of his trips with a large container of bouillabaisse that he picked up on the way back from the airport. I finished the first bowl and we still hadn't said much about anything. I sent out a feeler. "You know, I've lost a lot of weight. I don't think that place agrees with me."

He scraped out a mussel and tossed the shell on a plate. "Your mother and I talked it over and decided to start you in The American School of London next year. It's a long ride, but you'll be happier there."

Bouillabaisse gets better as it sits. I ladled out a second bowl. "This is really good."

Three

MGB

After vacationing on the Mediterranean in Calpi, Spain in 1967, we moved to Mountain Lakes, New Jersey. We bought a three-story stucco house built on a steep hill in the 1930s, and moved in on a day as hot as any in the south of Spain. My brother, sister, and I started school a few days after commencement.

Mountain Lakes was a car town. Seniors were allowed to drive to school. My classmates had their own cars. Bob Sanchez on the next block had a Citroen DS19; Brian Thompson across the street had an Austin Healey 3000; the captain of the football team had a Corvette Shark. My father joined the sports car madness and traded the Minx toward a blue MGB convertible with wire wheels. At first I had to drive my mother's Oldsmobile station wagon with a manual shift.

My English learner's permit was no good in the United States so I had to walk to school for the first few weeks, but when I got my New Jersey permit I could finally drive. Driving my mother's Oldsmobile with the shift on the column placed me low on the coolness scale, but this soon changed. I had taken lessons in a Morris Mini Minor driving on the left side of the road. Instead of looking left, right, left, before pulling out at a major intersection, I did it British style and looked right, left, right, and totaled the car. Fortunately, there were no injuries. The school newspaper ran a weekly series called "Demolition Derby" and I advanced to first place. There were several challengers to my title, but I held the lead for several editions until Randal Scott wrecked his Shelby and was hospitalized overnight with a broken leg and lacerations. His dad bought him a handmade sportscar with an ashwood frame called a Morgan to ease the pain.

Dad bought Mom a maroon Mercedes 230 Fin Tail to replace the Olds. I took my savings, and with a gift from my grandfather, bought a used VW Beetle that needed a little work. Mountain Lakes was close to New York City, so Dad drove the MG to Manhattan to manage his marketing madmen team.

Whenever we went anywhere as a family, he would take command of the Mercedes even though it was Mom's. One evening we went out to dinner. This was during a period of male menopause when dad talked about wishing he taught at a university and had not gone into marketing. My high school had sent out a questionnaire to the seniors asking about future career plans and which colleges we were interested in. My parents had never talked to me about what I wanted to be or which college I wanted to attend. I hadn't thought about it and didn't have a clue.

As we drove down the highway at dusk, I announced I wanted to join the Marine Corps. Dad launched into a dissertation about the history of the Vietnam War starting with Eisenhower. I can picture it clearly because the Mercedes had an ivory colored steering wheel. One hand let go of the wheel. Dad talked about the military-industrial complex, waving and pointing in the air for emphasis. He went through the Kennedy administration, then as he started on Johnson, the other hand released its grip. The car began drifting into the oncoming lane.

"Hey Dad, you're drifting," I said. The car was halfway over the double striped dividing line as he launched into the Gulf of Tonkin.

"You're in the wrong lane. Get over," Mom cried. Dad turned to her with a blank look on his face. "What? We're fine."

An oncoming car swerved to avoid us, horn blaring. We continued drifting. "Johnny, you're going to kill us," Mom screamed. White bones and skulls flew through the air as we all joined in. He calmly steered back onto our side of the highway. The sound of horns and squealing tires receded in the distance.

Mom's voice was broken, it was so high. "What's wrong with you, Johnny. You could have killed us!"

"Everything's fine. What?"

A week later Dad took me to a seminar by David Schoenbrun, a foreign correspondent known as one of Murrow's Boys who opposed the escalation of the war in Vietnam. The lecture convinced me not to join the Marines, but I remained uncertain about the point of going to college. My father had lived through the Great Depression and never had a doubt about his goals. But in my senior year I let my grades go. I told my parents I had no clue what profession to pursue. Dad set me up for aptitude testing in Philadelphia. I spent the afternoon taking more than aptitude tests. A psychologist interviewed me and gave me a Rorschach inkblot test and an IQ test. When they were done, I asked what the results were and what career I should pursue. I learned my

IQ was very high and they had nothing to recommend because I could succeed at anything I tried. Sure. That was when I realized I had the type of brain that got you into trouble: a dissenter's brain, one that saw things from a different perspective.

I wasn't going to be a success-driven over achiever. "What did I take the test for? It's useless," I said.

The doctor frowned. "You are an even balance between art and science."

"Isn't there anything you could recommend?"

"You might try architecture. Or mechanical engineering. You scored in the 99th percentile for mechanical aptitude."

Dad picked a small liberal arts college in Ohio for me called Defiance College. It was known as "the school on top of the hill." Hills in Ohio are ten feet high. It was an economical choice.

Somehow, I made it through the rest of twelfth grade. I dated a girl named Laura Wright and we were considered an item for a while. We went to local dances and sometimes did our homework together. I was about to ask her to go to the senior prom when she suddenly asked, "Do you love me?" I actually thought I did but answered in too great a detail: "I'm not sure. I'm too young to know what love is." Perhaps that is why *Lady Chatterley's Lover* was banned in the United States or perhaps I was guilty of information overload. She ditched me immediately.

Sherri Catalano and I were on friendly terms but didn't know one another well. I asked her to the prom at the last moment and she surprised me with a yes. Dad let me drive the MG, but by the time I filled it with gas and waxed it, I was late in picking her up. The corsage would not stay pinned on and she had to do it. It was awkward dancing with her and I felt like I didn't belong among the others who, like her, had shared their lives together for years. We both had a miserable time. I took her home early and knew there would not be a goodnight kiss as I walked her to the front door. "I'm sorry I ruined the evening," I said. "I'm maladjusted." She let herself in without replying.

Mom and Dad were still up when I got back. "You're home early," Dad remarked, "how did it go?"

He often would say to me, That is more than I need to know. Just boil it down. "Fine," I said, "the band was terrible." I threw the keys to him and went up to my room.

Dad, now forty, was promoted to manage IBM's major oil accounts. It was a high pressure, high visibility position. Somehow, he managed to pull the spokes lose from the steering wheel of the MG during the commute from Mountain Lakes to Manhattan. He drove it that way by holding on to the spokes until it could be replaced. Two months later we escaped from the hilly land of sportscars and trophy wives to Newtown, Pennsylvania, a few miles from Washington's Crossing Park.

Four

BUCKS COUNTY

Compared to most moves, it was a short puddle jump from New Jersey back to the Bucks County countryside. Dad considered Bucks County home and we were glad to be back, too. Our new house, built in 1738, stood in the middle of twenty acres of corn field. A metal silhouette sign at the driveway entrance proclaimed it to be Dolington Manor. The hand-fitted Pennsylvania blue-grey fieldstone walls were two feet thick. George Washington used it as an infirmary for his troops during the Revolutionary War and their blood stains remain in the wide plank floors today.

Dad researched the history of the property and entered it into the National Registry of Historic Homes. The land had been granted by William Penn to Benjamin Taylor. This was where Mom's antiques belonged. There were six fireplaces throughout the house. In the mahogany paneled study were rows of shelves which Dad filled with Hundred Percent Club sales trophies. The roof was cedar shake; it was like trying to heat the entire outdoors in the winter. The furnace never stopped running, but the seven-foot walk-in fireplace in the family room lent a warm ambience that took the chill off. On Sunday afternoons Dad read through the *New York Times* and scattered the pages over the floor in front of the fire. Burning embers popped over the screen and burned holes through the newspaper, but no amount of pleading broke him from this habit. We folded the pages for him and put them on the coffee table while he snored away on the couch.

My father's new position required little overnight travel during this period which lasted eleven years, the longest he ever stayed in one place. He commuted to Manhattan from Trenton, but occasionally worked in Princeton. Always true to Johnny Hopkins, he sometimes wore his Hopkins straw boater hat to work in Princeton.

I had trouble settling on a school and returned home to attend the local community college with no sense of direction, no idea of a career to pursue, or what I should major in. Mom and Dad didn't know what to do about my failure to launch. Dad put my mechanical aptitude to work waxing the floors, repairing shutters and windows, and cutting the eight acres of lawn. My maintenance abilities were exchanged for room and board. I read constantly, sometimes a couple books a week which included plays by Thorton Wilder, Shakespeare, and Moliere, and humanist works by Aldous Huxley and Alan Watts. I wrote a few sketches and taught myself the art of etching on sperm whale tooth ivory (scrimshandering) which I loved with a passion and placed for sale in nearby New Hope and nautical shops until the Endangered Species Act was passed in 1973.

During one of my sojourns at home Dad worked on a project in Princeton. On the way home from work he broke the MG's steering wheel again. I bought him a rally wheel with magnesium spokes for his birthday and installed it myself. I thought maybe the job pressure was finally getting to him and he took it out on the steering wheel. Shortly afterwards he broke the antenna and the tuner dial on the radio. The door handle snapped. Then he returned from Princeton with a mangled front fender. Dad told us it happened at an intersection on Main Street. "The policeman agreed with me it was the other guy's fault," he said.

Rather than fix the MG, he traded it in toward a mid-engine red Porsche 914 targa top. Just when he resumed work in New York, Dad was summoned to court and his license suspended. I drove him back and forth to the train station in Trenton, New Jersey, for several weeks. The Porsche came with Pirelli tires and refused to let go of the road. I left BMWs behind on the turns on the back roads of Bucks County.

At this time, he was taking on new accounts and under additional strain dealing with the world's largest petroleum companies. We were driving home from Trenton one evening and he was unusually quiet. Suddenly he said, "I was talking to Hess's brother and you know what he told me? 'You and your three-piece suits. I wouldn't buy anything from you if you were the only computer company on earth. You college boys think your shit smells good.'" He was only immune to pain on the outside. This pain registered on his face for days.

To relax, Dad joined the Porsche club at Holbert's Auto in Doylestown. On weekends the club practiced handling on a racetrack. One Saturday after practice, he came tearing down the driveway in a cloud of dust. The rear of the car bounced like it was on a pogo stick. I asked him how it happened, but he said he didn't know. The car spent three days at Holbert's for repairs. Both rear suspension struts were broken.

As the job pressure increased—so did his smoking. His diet did little to improve his blood pressure. He grilled steaks and hamburgers on the terrace at Dolington until they were crispy well done, then enjoyed a coffee and cigarette afterwards.

My brother came home from school to find him lying on his back in the family room turning blue. Mom stood over him holding the phone in her hand, shrieking. Jeff took the phone and called our family doctor, Howard Leister. Doctor Leister's office was a couple miles away. He came tearing down the drive, injected nitroglycerine, and called an ambulance before the dust settled to the ground.

It was a myocardial infarction, unusual for someone in their late forties. Dr. Leicester said that years of long commutes, high stress, smoking, and a family history of heart trouble, had led to the attack. After Dad's discharge from the hospital he was examined by an IBM doctor and forced to take an administrative position in Philadelphia where there was no pressure. Dad complained constantly and attempted to get his old position back, but the company doctor blocked it. He was told this was the new reality. Get used to it. Being told what to do was like being buried alive.

There was an epiphany. Dad changed his diet, took up swimming, shed pounds, and subscribed to a vitamin magazine. He let go of the Porsche club and resigned from the zoning board. By following a healthy regimen for several months, he returned to a reasonable state of fitness. Then with a stroke of brilliance inspired by desperation, Dad arranged for a transfer to Paris through his previous World Trade connections. He was free of the company doctor and the home office in White Plains at last. In the early spring, before moving to France, he and my mother bought a condominium in the newly built Henlopen in Rehoboth, Delaware, and furnished it with shore décor. It was an investment and a future home base for my parents to return to from Europe and for reuniting our scattered clan.

I dropped out of college again and moved in with my future wife, Deborah Call, who lived in Delran, New Jersey. In March our son, Justin was born. Dolington Manor was put up for sale and Mom and Dad moved to Le Vésinet in the suburbs of Paris in May of 1977.

The house in Le Vésinet was a three-story white stucco with a wrought iron fence and tall gates at each end of a circular drive. They moved in on a broiling hot day and the moving crew took a long lunch break. When the movers returned in the afternoon they were intoxicated. A large maple armoire destined for the second-floor master bedroom was too big to bring up the stairs. It was decided to haul it up through the bedroom balcony window, but their rope was too short. A ladder was brought up from the basement and leaned against the house. The armoire was strapped to the back of a fellow the size of Andre the Giant and a bottle of wine passed to him. He took several swallows, uttered an oath, then started up. At the halfway point, the ladder groaned and swayed dangerously, and he froze. A heated debate ensued. "Ne vous arrêtez pas maintenant, vous dupe - don't stop now, you fool," the supervisor said. Shaking with strain, the mover continued upward until the crew at the top could lean over the rails and grab the straps to pull the furniture inside.

My widowed grandmother, Georgia Groves, had come with them to live and was given the bedroom on the third floor. Mom brought her dogs along too; a poodle named Jolie and a miniature dachshund named Hildegard, who were quarantined for the first three months. The yard had a large vegetable garden which Mom and Dad split in half. Mom grew herbs and spices; Dad grew lettuce, eggplant, and spinach.

Mom and Dad loved France. Both took French lessons. Dad already spoke enough French to get along but wanted to be fluent enough to conduct business. They explored along the Dordogne to Vichy and made trips to the Côte d'Azur and Antibes, Marseilles, Nice and through the countryside of Province. My mother noted in her journal, *John enjoyed the topless beach at Bors very much*. At the Grand Prix in Monaco, they rooted for Mario Andretti and caught a glimpse of Princess Grace Kelly.

Dad traveled extensively behind the Iron Curtain. He called it pioneer marketing. The communist nations developed and installed a fraction of the computers that Western Europe and America had. Many of their data systems were based on reverse engineered IBM 360s, but COMCON, a Soviet-led economic alliance in Eastern Bloc countries (Poland, East Germany, Czechoslovakia, Hungary, Yugoslavia, Romania, Bulgaria, Albania) had instituted regulations to keep the West out. Their hardware was incompatible with the rest of the world, making it impossible for them to interface and therefore sell to western markets. The USSR was in a period of economic struggle known as the Brezhnevian Stagnation. IBM World Trade Corporation saw an opportunity to penetrate an untapped market.

Mom came along on some of the Iron Curtain trips. They went to Ljubljana Yugoslavia together. Dad spent several days at IBM Division Yugoslavia Intertrade and she explored the department stores and looked for a museum which she never found. The shops and stores weren't well-stocked like the ones in Paris and everything was more expensive. Dad met fellow IBMers in Yugoslavia and learned how countries under Tito conducted commerce. Bull SAS® of France had made sales in Czechoslovakia where there was a new openness toward western technology. The competitive Yugoslav IBMers arranged to hold business planning sessions there in the fall.

From Ljubljana my parents drove to Vienna. After taking in the wine district and eating at the home where Beethoven lived in 1817, they watched the Lipizzaner Horses perform beneath crystal chandeliers in their equestrian hall. They took the autobahn through the Black Forest to Baden Baden and stayed a few days at a health resort with thermal baths before returning to Le Vésinet. After resting over the weekend, Dad flew to Finland on Monday. On Tuesday, Holland. Mom spent time in St. Germain and Le Vésinet shopping for gifts and things for entertaining. Wednesday he was back for an evening soirée with some of their French friends. Thursday they attended a charity auction at Chateau Sceaux. By the end of their first three months in Europe they were exhausted. In August they flew back to The States for vacation.

Lydia and Glenn, Jeffrey, Deborah and I went down to the Henlopen for a family reunion. Debbie and I showed off our recently arrived son, Justin. Mom and Dad gave him a Spanish night gown and blanket. It was a one-piece linen gown with a lace neck. "We're going to nickname him Sweet Pea," I said. "Like in Popeye the Sailor and Olive Oyle."

Justin had been born with Heinlein Membrane Disease, a sometimes fatal respiratory disorder that required an oxygenated sterile isolette and constant monitoring at Pennsylvania Hospital for the beginning weeks of his life, but he recovered fully. He was the first of many grandchildren. Being first has its advantages. Debbie wrapped him in his new blanket. Mom pointed to herself. "Mor Mor." Debbie handed him over and he blew spit bubbles.

Dad gave out babushka nesting dolls and Hungarian hand-painted wooden shingles, glancing impatiently at my mother from time to time. "What do you want to be called, Dad?" Jeff asked.

"Poppi." He gave Debbie her present and held out his arms for the baby.

"What about plain Grandmom and Grandpop?" I said. "We aren't Scandinavian."

Mom relinquished Justin. "We're going to be Mor Mor and Poppi,"

I was overruled.

We had get-togethers off and on for the duration of Dad's vacation, a period of about nine weeks. During this time Mom and Dad visited friends and relatives in Sinking Springs and Bucks County, Pennsylvania. Then they returned to Le Vésinet. Every three or four months they returned to The States for eight or nine weeks. The cycle repeated for three years. In March of 1980, Dad's Paris assignment ended. The first two years had been exhilarating, but the last year of constant travel had taken a toll and he was anxious to go home.

Debbie and I were married for two years when the expats returned. They decided to keep the condominium as a summer house and to settle in Bucks County. They stayed with us in our new townhouse in Quakertown, then circulated between my brother and sister for a few weeks until they found a nineteenth-century brick house on the Delaware in Kitnersville. They rented there for six months while their own house was built in a development on the river called Bridlewood. At Bridlewood we feasted on cassolettes, beef bourguignon, minestrone, hand turned sorbets and ice cream, and homemade breads and noodles made from scratch with techniques learned in cooking classes in Le Vésinet. All served with good French wines stocked in Dad's wine cave.

Five

LIES AND INNUENDOS

The American golden age of business took a tumble. In 1984, under an agreement with the federal government reached in 1982 regarding anti-trust laws, Ma Bell (AT&T) and other corporations were forced to split up into smaller companies or close divisions. I made my career in upstart technologies such as mini and microcomputers and networking, struggling to compete against the giant IBM Corporation which had installed half the world's computers. Despite being at opposite ends of the computer spectrum, Dad and I drove together to a technology fair in New York and spent the afternoon looking at the tiny new computers, network routers, and communications gear. I think he could feel the world changing again and sense the paradigm shift. I was working for a company called "Computers for the Professional" in Valley Forge as Advanced Technologies Manger when IBM announced it would self-regulate before the government decided to break it up for them. IBM split voluntarily into smaller subsidiaries. Shortly after, huge losses were announced. Big Blue outsourced manufacturing, ended the production of mainframes, and laid off employees. Dad was forced into early retirement at age fifty-five, along with thousands of others.

Lydia held a retirement party and I hired a barbershop quartet called "The Young at Hearts" to sing. Their tenor died two days before the party. They were one short but performed anyway. It was held outside with a dining tent and catered dinner. About thirty friends and relatives came. When everyone found a seat, Dad stood in front of The Young at Hearts. He tapped his spoon on his glass and announced, "I'm not retiring." He had formed J. T. Brown Consulting, incorporated in the tax haven of Delaware. They were moving to Lewes across the Delaware Bay from Rehoboth.

His energy had returned. He and Mom put up for sale the Bridlewood house and the condominium. For their next home, they contracted Jack Vessels and David Dunbar of Lewestown Restorations to move a historic barn in Sussex County, Delaware, to Shipcarpenter Square in Lewes. The barn was restored and an addition larger than the original barn added.

The sale of the two homes provided startup capital. Mom opened her own business called The Celtic Pavilion, located behind King's Ice Cream in Lewes. She and Dad, mostly of Irish and Scottish ancestry respectively, made trips to Ireland and the Hebrides to buy goods and hand-woven clothes to stock the store. Dad commuted to New Jersey and New York to conduct information planning sessions for Fortune 100 companies. One project involved consulting in Paris for a petroleum company which flew him and my mother from JFK to Charles de Gaulle Airport in three hours on the Concorde Super Sonic Transport (SST). The White Bird, as it was nicknamed, flew at nearly twice the speed of sound. Mom said it was too noisy.

Being in business for yourself turned out to be lucrative, but Dad didn't forget the lessons he learned working at his grandfather's delicatessen. He rode the wave of success for four years, then wound down the business and took up community service. Officially retired in 1993, he juggled his time between Rector's and Accounting Warden of St. John's Episcopal Church; president of the Lewes chapters of Habitat for Humanity and the Lions Club; and Lewes Chamber of Commerce Executive Director. To name a few.

My parents planted roses around the house and tried to grow a lawn in the sandy soil and summer heat of the shore community. A local gardener was hired to come once a week. During the second fall, the man didn't show up for over a week. Dad walked from Shipcarpenter Square to his home, a few blocks away, and knocked on the door. The wife let him in. Her husband lay on a cot in the living room, asleep. It was a cold day and there was no heat in the house. It's a brain tumor, she told him. He had a couple of months to live at best.

Dad brought in the Lions Club. The Lions repaired the furnace and paid for the fuel oil through the winter until he died.

Lewes was a long drive from Bucks County, Pennsylvania where my sister, brother, and I were caught in our own struggles raising our families during the recession of 1979 and adjusting to the new economic reality of stagflation that followed for years. Spam casserole and beans and franks were staples of our diet. Dad's business seemed unaffected. I changed jobs several times due to buyouts, layoffs, and bankruptcies. The golden age of post war American boom and the reign of the IBM Big Iron was not there for us, but despite that, we did well enough. Our families grew. Justin had a new sister, Lindsay, and new brother, Russel. Lydia and Glenn had two sons in quick succession, Ian and Collin. Jeff and his wife, Barbara, grew their branch of the family and added Jeffrey Joel, Kathryn, James, and Rachel to the clan. We were breeders. Like most breeders, we got caught up in the endless whirl of teacher – parent conferences, school plays, band, Sunday school, baseball, soccer, and trips to the doctor. Lindsay and Jeffrey Joel broke their arms, Russel bit his tongue half off, Collin had an operation on his intestines. James had Crohn's Disease.

Mom and Dad drove up to stay with us for a few days when Justin turned twelve. We lived in a little farmhouse on Thatcher Road in Richland, near where Sterner's Mill now lies beneath Lake Nockamixon. Lindsay was six, and Russel five.

The house on Thatcher Road was out in the country. Most of our neighbors kept horses and next door to us they allowed ducks and sheep inside their home. We woke to roosters crowing. When the wind blew a certain way, we were enveloped in barnyard odors. There was a guy whom we passed almost daily walking alongside his pet cow on the back roads on their way into town. He would park his cow in a parking spot at Dunkin'® Donuts in Quakertown while he went in for coffee and donuts. The locals called him "Tex." It was as far away from Europe as you could get.

"Your father and I have an idea," Mom said.

She often had good ideas. I smiled playfully. "That could be dangerous."

Dad was wrestling with a roast in the oven that had slid out of the pan and splattered *au jus* everywhere. "Don't be disrespectful to your mother."

It was like a fake knife lunge. "I'm not. I'm joking - jeese."

Debbie opened the kitchen window to let the smoke out, then came to my mother's aid. "We're listening. What is it?"

"We want to take our grandchildren to Europe."

"All of them?" said Debbie.

The smoke in the room thinned and the oven fire was safely under control. "A couple at a time, by age when they are old enough," said Dad. "Justin and Ian are old enough. I'll show you the itinerary after dinner. We have a place reserved in Vorms for two weeks this summer. Next summer we'll take the girls. After that, Russel, Jeffrey Joel, and Collin. We think all the kids should have a chance to see Europe."

"How are you traveling - by train?" I said.

"We'll rent a car. Your mother and I will take turns driving." Debbie and I exchanged glances.

The plan involved revisiting many of the places they had been when they lived in Le Vésinet plus the prehistoric caves of Lascaux and the Pont du Gard Roman aqueduct bridge. He was the manager. Always in charge. It was difficult to imagine him giving up control of the wheel.

"We wanted to do this for a long time." said Mom.

The pros outweighed the cons and the children were all for it. As Mark Twain said in *The Innocents Abroad*, "Travel is fatal to prejudice, bigotry, and narrow-mindedness, and many of our people need it sorely on these accounts. Broad, wholesome, charitable views of men and things cannot be acquired by vegetating in one little corner of the earth all one's lifetime."

Debbie and I consented with a twinge of jealousy since we were not included. In reality, it took longer than expected to complete the plan. England, Scotland, and Wales were added to the itinerary. James was juggled in when he was feeling better. After each trip we questioned the children about where they had been and what they had seen. Glowing descriptions of cave paintings, mineral springs, castles, and swimming in the Dordogne to cool off from the heat, left no doubt that they loved these adventures. But over time, a growing body of evidence grew that we were not being told everything.

My mother was the first to crack. After living in Lewes for fifteen years, Mom and Dad sold the barn house and had a house built in Ottsville, Pennsylvania to be closer to the rest of their children. They had strewn wildflower seeds in the surrounding field and called it La Pâquerette. We were invited for dinner. Dad was ladling out fish chowder he had made and the conversation had gotten around to their trip to St. Ciprian in Dordogne with Russel, Collin, and Jeffrey Joel.

"Your father almost drowned me," Mom said.

"You're not getting any." Dad put the tureen down.

"It's true. Poppi stood up in the canoe and turned it over," said Russ.

Debbie picked up the tureen and filled Mom's bowl. "Come on, Mom. What happened?"

"The boys took kayaks and your father and I had a canoe. We were on the Vergie River and left from Les Egglies de Tayoc. About an hour and a half later a great storm came up with lightning and thunder and great drops of rain. And we were in the middle of the river. The banks were high with rocks and trees, so we had no choice but to take the river during the lightning. Jeff's kayak was filling up with water and wouldn't keep on course. We did finally make it to Les Egglies but only it was the wrong dock. Then your father stood up..."

"Lies. Lies and innuendo!"

"Come on, Poppi, confess," said Russ.

"He overturned the canoe. My purse, our money, and camera all fell in."

"Don't listen to her. It's not true."

"It took days to dry everything out. Maybe someday we'll laugh about it."

That was the first crack in the dam, and it was widening. I looked around the table to Lindsay and Justin. Lindsay was smiling.

I tilted my head. "Anything else we should know about?"

"There was the time the car got stuck in the ditch in Scotland."

"St. Patrick's Church in Carlyle," said Mom.

"There was a music festival at the church and Poppi parked the car across the street on the side of a hill. It rained while we were inside. When we came out the car had slid to the bottom in the mud and got stuck. The choir came out and tied a rope to the bumper and pulled us out."

"They were the nicest people," said Mother.

Justin kept it in, but something was brewing. He didn't want to rat on his grandfather right in front of him, but a few days later, he let loose when he was back home. In Province, Dad had bought baguettes, cheese and wine at a country store. They drove through a local park looking for a place to have lunch. The dirt road led through woods until it dead ended. Two trees blocked the way to an open field of lavender, a perfect place to eat and enjoy the view.

"The space was narrow, but Poppi thought he could make it. It sounded like fingernails on a chalk board. Then the car stuck solid. Poppi put it in reverse but the wheels just spun. We tried pushing it backwards, but it was wedged tight."

"How did you get it out?" I asked.

"Some hikers came across the field and pushed us back through. Everyone had a big laugh, then Poppi thanked them with a bottle of wine."

Six

TOO COLD FOR BUTTERFLIES

More stories followed. Too many to tell. They are part of our family legends. There were more moves; one to Erwinna, Pennsylvania near Van Sant Glider Port, one to an L-shaped French architectural design with a seventeen-pitch roof and French doors and windows in Carversville, Pennsylvania. The Carversville house they named Bois Joli, pretty woods. Then the wanderlust ebbed out. My parents built an in-law-suite onto Lydia and Glenn's house across the street from Our Lady of Mount Carmel Cemetery in Doylestown Pennsylvania. "That is our next move," Mom joked.

Dad made their funeral arrangements. A new will was drawn up and copies distributed to the immediate family. Written instructions for his funeral were given to my sister that included a reception and a piper to play Skye Boat Song at his burial. He was a MacMillan with the kilts to prove it. Investments, contacts, and household inventory were classified and stored in colored dividers with printed labels and placed in order in his desk drawer.

My father had a neat bold hand that was unmistakable, but by the spring of 2013 it had deteriorated to hen scratch. He couldn't write the checks to pay the bills. Mom gave him a pen: a six hundred fifty-dollar William Henry 1207 Chablis with a Box Elder Burl wood barrel and a pocket clip set with smoky quartz. The checks were still unreadable. Neither the pen nor love could fix that.

He showed remarkable will power to the end, which did not turn out to be gracious the way he planned. It took many things to kill Dad. The downturn began when he took his dog for his usual walk one evening. Dad was hit by a pickup truck crossing the intersection a few blocks from home. Gus was a pedigreed show dog registered as Gus the Griffon, Champion JW Top Gun of Tidewater, and was a rising star in national dog shows. Ironically, Gus was hit by a pickup, too, a few years before. Dad had a titanium rod inserted in his back leg to save him. He was nuts about the dog and covered his study walls with pictures of him. Gus recovered but that was the end of his career as a show dog.

My sister, Lydia, told it to us this way: Daddy walked through the front door as usual, but the dog was shaking.

"What's wrong with Gus?" The dog started to whine. The way she explained it, a policeman rang the doorbell a moment later and said Dad was knocked down by a pickup truck while crossing the street, but before he could get any information Dad got up and walked away.

"Let me call an ambulance," the policeman told her. Gus kept whining.

"I don't need one," Dad snapped.

"Are you sure you're okay?" Lydia asked.

"My leg hurts. But I'm fine."

"Let me take a look," said the policemen.

"Take your pants down, Daddy," Lydia ordered.

The bone was showing beneath the skin. He refused an ambulance. They forced him into his car, and she drove him to the ER where X-rays revealed a broken femur requiring a full leg cast.

After Dad got the cast off, Mom tripped on a rug and broke her pelvis. Dad drove to the rehab center every day to spend the afternoon with her. Returning home one night he couldn't turn on the lamp sitting on the cabinet in the living room. The circuit breaker panel was in the basement and the stairs were narrow and steep. The five bottom steps had no handrail and that's where he fell off, grabbing at shelves crammed with glass canning jars and pulling them down with him. He struck his head on a steel support column on his way down to the floor.

Dad was partly conscious when Lydia got to him. She called an ambulance and he was taken to Doylestown Hospital, then flown to Jefferson in Philadelphia. He had bleeding on the brain. And another complication, MRSA, a staph infection resistant to antibiotics that is usually transmitted by hospital personnel.

I had taken advantage of a better job opportunity in the South and moved my family from Richland, Pennsylvania to Richmond, Virginia. It usually took six hours to drive back up to Doylestown. I made good time getting to my parents' place and immediately entered their in-law-suite. Nothing was wrong with the lamp that caused Dad to go down to the basement. A wall switch had been turned off by mistake. My sister, brother, and I drove to Jefferson and visited. Outside his room his neurologist told us they expected to need to operate to relieve the pressure on his brain. After we suited up for MRSA we were allowed to enter.

A nurse came in to check on him. Dad told her that he was in very good shape and exercised regularly. Then he said,

"I don't need an operation. I'm a manager." I was perplexed as to why he believed being a manager in the past made a difference. Whether he was confused or not was a moot question. The bleeding stopped the next day and resorbed on its own.

When we got back to Doylestown, I spoke with my mother. She told me he had been making fun of her at breakfast. I asked her to explain.

"He made funny sounds at me. Sometimes nothing came out. I don't know why he was so mean to me."

I exhaled slowly. "Mom, that's a stroke."

When he returned home ten days later, Lydia handed him a booklet from Jefferson Hospital entitled: "So You've Had a Stroke." On the front was a picture of a Father Knows Best actor in a wheelchair pushed by a nurse. Dad crumpled it up and threw it in the trash. "I didn't have a stroke."

She had the doctor fax the medical report to her and held it up in front of his face. Written across the page in Magic Marker was STROKE in capitals.

There were attempts to find Dad a rehabilitation center where he felt comfortable. He was transferred several times but hated them all. He said nasty things about people and seemed to have undergone a personality change but that was probably the Gabapentin anti-seizure medication. We had his dosage cut in half and he returned to himself again. He was released and came home, but two days later became delirious and had hallucinations. Doylestown Hospital diagnosed him with a urinary tract infection and experimented for a week with different catheters and antibiotics to find the combination that could clear it up. Once back home, he developed a bacterial lung infection caused by a swallowing disorder and was readmitted to the hospital. Cycles of urinary and lung infections recurred for many iterations.

Mom came home, then Dad. We rearranged the furniture so they could maneuver their walkers around the house. Caregivers were hired but as far as my mother was concerned, they could do nothing right. She underwent her own personality change and insulted and berated one of the care workers so badly the home care company pulled them and said not to ever call again. This took a toll on Lydia. She was busy running an industrial supply company with my brother-in-law, Glenn, and now spent much of her time picking up medical supplies and driving my parents to doctors' appointments. I came up from Richmond for a week or two at a time so she and Glenn could get away for a while.

While staying in Doylestown I finished writing a story about our Finnish family friends called "Breaking Them with Words." I signed it J. T. Brown and gave it to my father to read. Dad was an avid reader. I grew up reading the best sellers with which he filled our bookshelves. *Minister of Death*, *The Godfather*, and *Portnoy's Complaint* were some of my favorites. He loved poetry, too, and would take a book of poems down from the shelf after Sunday dinner to read to us. He had a sonorous voice and often recited Poe's "Eldorado" by heart. Nothing fit him better.

He handed the manuscript back the next day. "I don't like it."

I know I've written some bad stuff before, but I was hoping for criticism that was more specific. "What don't you like about it?"

"I just don't."

Two weeks later, Dad asked me not to sign my writing using J. T. Brown. He was worried about his legacy.

I snarked back: "I didn't ask for my name. You gave it to me." But he was the head of the clan and it was an order. The story was published signed as J. Thomas.

He had another urinary tract infection, then fell and broke his hip. I visited him at Doylestown Hospital and his demeanor was poor. He said quietly, "I'm afraid of dying."

I never felt more inadequate in my life. No words of solace or comfort came to mind. "No one has ever come back to talk about it," was the best I came up with. I sat by his bedside, feeling the weight of the silence. "Would you like me to get the priest?"

He nodded imperceptibly. I drove to the church and she was out at a function, but she did visit him the next morning. Dad was active with the church and she knew him well. Whatever they talked about, it did not relieve him of his fears.

The squamous cell cancer in his lungs and esophagus was found far too late and he was very frail. It was probably there all along disguised by the other ailments, but he never complained. I wondered if it was something he couldn't feel like the prong in his toe or the broken leg. The heart center called to ask his permission to turn off the Medtronic defibrillator-pacemaker that was implanted years before as the result of the heart attack at Dolington. It had accidentally shocked him several times setting it up in the beginning, causing much pain, but his heart was very bad and it was an unquestionable necessity. He gave his consent and the hospital sent out a technician to neutralize it by passing a magnetic device over his chest. My sister, brother, and I stood by his bedside. The technician shut off the transmitter. He bent over Dad to de-activate the implant.

"Does it have to be now?" Dad asked.

"It's going to set off all kinds of alarms back at the heart center when it goes off, Mr. Brown. You don't want that to happen, do you?"

"I need to think about it more."

Will power. I had it too. The autonomous system takes over. You still breathe anyway. I locked my knees to keep from falling. "You already agreed, Dad. It has to be done. You remember what it's like when that thing goes off. One more time and it will kill you."

Debbie and I spent New Years Eve and the next week with Dad, Mom, Lydia, and Glenn. On the 24th of January, 2014, I was back in Richmond when Jeff called. "Mom says it's going to be today. She said that the last time, but maybe it is."

I left right away when my brother called, but at 3 p.m. got stuck on Route 95 below Philadelphia. I called to let them know I was in a miles long traffic jam. The Christmas tree still was up with the decorations on in Mom and Dad's living room in Doylestown. Dad's hospice bed had been placed in the middle so he could be with everyone. My brother-in-law held the phone and I told Dad I loved him.

"You can let go, Dad. We'll all be fine."

He told me he loved me. I missed his death by half an hour. Soon after I arrived, Glenn told me he was holding Dad's hand when he died. "Your Dad said: 'My four brothers are standing over there, see them.' I thought he had two brothers, not four."

"Two brothers and a sister, Beverly, who died when she was five. I don't know what he was seeing, Glenn."

The math doesn't matter. Perhaps it was a hallucination caused by the urinary tract infection or the cancer. I was glad he found a way to let go.

The night after Dad passed, I sat at his desk collecting things for his obituary and funeral service. The desk sat at a window overlooking the entrance to the backyard. On the gate is a chime that plays a melody when the wind blows or the gate opens. I logged into Dad's laptop and found photos of Maasai villagers and the pump station he helped build by directing a collaboration of the Doylestown and Langata, Kenya, Rotary Clubs. As I sort through the photos the chime plays. I continue sorting and the melody plays again. It's a still January night, far too cold for butterflies. The backyard is empty.

After Dad's burial, Mom gave me his William Henry pen and his most prized possession, a Maasai hand carved wooden staff covered in tightly woven beads presented to him for his leadership in building water wells for Langata, Kenya.

I was fortunate to be able to spend time with him during his last year. He told me how in 2011 he coordinated the project of the Langata Kenya Rotary and the Doylestown Rotary to raise funds to build water wells and a pump house for a Maasai village. The women had to walk miles to carry water from a water hole in urns balanced on their heads. The pumping station would provide safe, clean water, but it required pipes to pass through a neighboring tribe's land. They refused to allow it. Dad said he didn't think it would happen, but it did. It took two years to negotiate the settlement between the tribes. He said to me, "You can't imagine how deeply satisfying it is to be able to help people in that way. It was the most rewarding thing in my life."

It is difficult for me to understand why he struggled so hard against letting go of life. It is said that sometimes wanderlust is caused by a desire to escape guilt. I would not know what that could be. Maybe he felt there was something left undone. But the truth is, we loved him as much for his faults as his accomplishments. There is one more thing to tell. A year after Dad died, I had a vivid dream about him. A visitation.

I was walking a long corridor filled with people all moving in the same direction. Everything was bright and distinct. No matter how hard I tried to walk faster, everyone kept passing me. I grew cold, weaker, and older with each footstep. Then someone put something in my pants pockets. I shoved in my hands and felt Laplander mittens. The ones I was given for Christmas as a boy. I could see every fine fiber of wool and floated between the fibers, feeling their deep warmth and comfort flow through me. I looked to my side and there was Dad walking along with me. He was my father as I knew him in his early thirties.

"Dad, is that you?"

Terror struck me when he turned into a corpse. Then, in a split second he became himself in his prime again. He wanted to show me he was dead.

"Dad, are you alright? Is everything okay?" Meaning, in death.

He became extremely animated and spoke very rapidly, but no sound came from his lips. Dad was trying to express great joy and awe, but there are no words to describe what he now knows.

We walked along together. The corridor filled with bright light. A doorway opened at the end and a cold clean wind blew through me. I awoke in my bed in Richmond remembering the dream in detail.

ABOUT THE AUTHOR

J. Thomas Brown's short stories have appeared in Scarlet Leaf Review and Everywhere Stories: Short Fiction from a Small Planet. He has contributed poems to Lingering in the Margins: A River City Poets Anthology.

OTHER WORKS

Mooncalf, a poetry collection

Land of Three Houses, historical fiction

The Hole in the Bone, historical fantasy

St. Elmo's Light, a short story collection

To connect with the author, please visit www.jthomasbrown.com

www.ingramcontent.com/pod-product-compliance
Lightning Source LLC
Chambersburg PA
CBHW071416290426
44108CB00014B/1842